TOOLS FOR TEACHERS

- **ATOS:** 0.7
- **GRL:** C
- **LEXILE:** 150L

- **CURRICULUM CONNECTIONS:** animals
- **WORD COUNT:** 57

Skills to Teach

- **HIGH-FREQUENCY WORDS:** a, do, its, see, the, you
- **CONTENT WORDS:** digs, ears, eyes, hides, hooves, listens, looks, mouth, nurses, piglet, sniffs, snout, tail, wiggles
- **PUNCTUATION:** periods, question marks
- **WORD STUDY:** silent *t* (*listens*); /z/, spelled *s* (*eyes*), *es* (*hooves*, *nurses*, *wiggles*); *r*-controlled vowels (*ears*, *nurses*); long /i/, spelled *eye* (*eyes*), *i_e* (*hides*); short /oo/ (*hooves*); dipthong /ou/ (*mouth*)
- **TEXT TYPE:** information report

Before Reading Activities

- Read the title and give a simple statement of the main idea.
- Have students "walk" though the book and talk about what they see in the pictures.
- Introduce new vocabulary by having students predict the first letter and locate the word in the text.
- Discuss any unfamiliar concepts that are in the text.

After Reading Activities

List the different parts of a piglet, such as eyes, hooves, snout, and tail, on the board. Encourage children to consider which farm babies (lambs, foals, calves, etc.) might have the same parts, and if so, how they are similar or different. Does a calf have a tail? Is it curly? How about a chick? Following the children's suggestions, write the animal's name underneath the body part.

Tadpole Books are published by Jump!, 5357 Penn Avenue South, Minneapolis, MN 55419, www.jumplibrary.com

Copyright ©2018 Jump. International copyright reserved in all countries. No part of this book may be reproduced in any form without written permission from the publisher.

Editor: Jenny Fretland VanVoorst **Designer:** Anna Peterson

Photo Credits: Dreamstime: Tsekhmister, 4–5. Getty: James Southworth/EyeEm, 2–3; DLILLC/Corbis/VCG, 12–13. iStock: GlobalP, 1; JHJR, 9. Shutterstock: Sonsedska Yuliia, cover; multiart, 8; Sven Hoppe, 10–11; YanaGr, 14–15. SuperStock: NaturePL, 6–7.

Library of Congress Cataloging-in-Publication Data
Names: Mayerling, Tim.
Title: Piglets / by Tim Mayerling.
Description: Minneapolis, Minnesota: Jump!, Inc., 2017. | Series: Farm babies | Audience: Age 3–6. | Includes index.
Identifiers: LCCN 2017013116 (print) | LCCN 2017005144 (ebook) | ISBN 9781624966156 (ebook) | ISBN 9781620317686 (hardcover: alk. paper) | ISBN 9781620317884 (pbk.)
Subjects: LCSH: Piglets—Juvenile literature. | Swine—Juvenile literature.
Classification: LCC SF395.5 (print) | LCC SF395.5 .M39 2017 (ebook) | DDC 636.4/07—dc23
LC record available at https://lccn.loc.gov/2017013116LC record available at https://lccn.loc.gov/2016058409

FARM BABIES

PIGLETS

by Tim Mayerling

TABLE OF CONTENTS

tadpole
books

A piglet looks.

Do you see
its eyes?

A piglet listens.

Do you see
its ears?

A piglet sniffs.

snout

Do you see its snout?

A piglet digs.

hooves

Do you see
its hooves?

A piglet nurses.

Do you see its mouth?

A piglet wiggles.

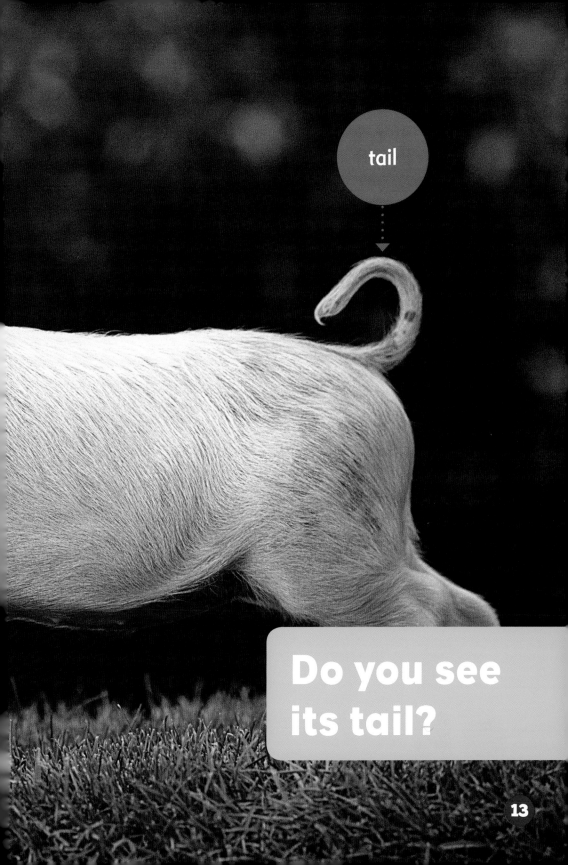

tail

Do you see its tail?

A piglet hides.

Do you see
the piglet?

WORDS TO KNOW

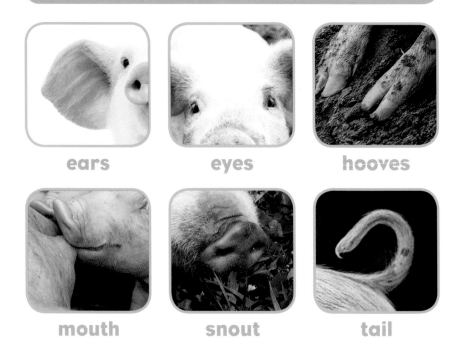

ears   eyes   hooves

mouth   snout   tail

INDEX